ROW BY ROW

Also by the Author:
Gleanings from a Well-Watered Garden
Buckets

ROW

BY

ROW

a crop of thoughts from a New Hampshire farm

By

Jane W. Lauber

THE GOLDEN QUILL PRESS
Publishers
Francestown   New Hampshire

© JANE W. LAUBER 1988

Library of Congress Catalog Card Number 88-80079

ISBN 0-8233-0445-0

Printed in the United States of America

Dedication

To "Dearie"
  (Lucile W. Sharp), my precious grandmother—
  now in His glory—and hers—
  who taught me the love of beauty and growing things,
  the love of Truth,
  and most of all,
  the love of God.

ACKNOWLEDGEMENTS

Scripture quotations marked (RSV) are from *The Revised Standard Version* of the Bible. Old Testament Section, copyright 1952, by Division of Christian Education of the National Council of the Churches of Christ in the United States of America. New Testament Section, copyright 1946 by Division of Christian Education of the National Council of the Churches of Christ in the United States of America.

Scripture quotation marked (NEB) is from *The New English Bible*, copyright by The Delegates of the Oxford University Press and The Syndics of the Cambridge University Press 1961, 1970.

Scripture quotations marked (AMP) are from *The Amplified Bible.* Old Testament copyright 1965, 1987 by the Zondervan Corporation. The Amplified New Testament copyright 1958, 1987 by The Lockman Foundation.

CONTENTS

Introduction

This New England to which Burt and I have come, is a wonderfully graphic land, layered with lovely legends and legacies of her past with their illustrated pages of winding stone walls, gnarled antique apple trees, overgrown lilac hedges, classically proportioned homes and artistically crafted furnishings and implements. All of these teach us of this land's lavish history and her inventive and intrepid people.

Nature, herself, is an apt teacher here. Our farm life necessitates a close, "kissing kin" relationship with her, and she, through sign and simile shows us many truths of her creation and Creator.

Of course she always has. Scripture is full of references to Nature's images as symbolic graphics of God's truth, such as our being called "the sheep of his pasture," the Spirit being described as "rivers of living water," and hundreds upon hundreds more. But here in New England, the lessons relating to the four seasons, Nature teaches with particular emphasis. For here the seasons are high drama, enacted with full operatic voices, and demanding of the audience strict attention and subsequent action. To ignore the lessons of the seasons is peril, but to heed and savor them is delight.

Many are the symbols with the seasons, but one I would suggest is that in them each year, Nature portrays a minicycle of God's great Drama—His cosmic tale, His "holy history" or "Heilig Geschichete," as the Germans call it. I see Nature suggesting, through each season's images, the major episodes in God's masterful man-plan, in fact I see God painting His own artistic illustrations for His "Heilig Geschichete."

I watch as God paints springtime at our farm. I see new life rising from the brown, dead earth with fresh pastel greens in our meadows and delicate pinks in the swelling buds of our woodlands. He swirls yellow greens on the fiddle-head ferns, curling upward into life along the banks of our beaver pond, and white blossoms are brushed across the weathered grey limbs of the old apple orchard. I am awed by the new life being birthed in our barn—the fuzzy white lambs, the comical dancing goat kids, and the frolicking wide-eyed calves. We watch energetic seedlings emerge from the seed Burt has planted in our vegetable gardens. Death has given way to life—and the world seems "born again!"

During this same season, Burt and I with other Christians, gather on Bear Hill overlooking Hillsboro, to watch the sunrise, to celebrate and sing, "Christ the Lord is risen today, Hallelujah!" Good Friday's services are past, death has given way to life, and the triumphant message of Spring and Scripture is sounded—that new life, new birth—all new beginnings are made possible through the death and resurrection of Jesus Christ!

This season also, the "early rains" arrive to water our seeds, plantings and fields. So too, we celebrate Pentecost, when the "early rains" of the Holy Spirit fell upon the Church to water the seeds and plantings of God, and to provide the power to grow, to develop, and to overcome.

Summer arrives in New England with its luxurious emerald landscapes and flourishing multi-colored gardens of vegetables and flowers which God strokes generously on His canvas. Here I see portrayed the growth process of the Church as individually, God's people must assimilate the nourishments, receive the waterings and endure the weedings and pruning of God's cultivation process— always orienting toward the Light, that maturity and usefulness may be achieved.

I watch an indescribably vivid New England Fall appear on the canvas of God. The mountains and hills seem to "break forth. . .into singing" and the trees of the field seem to "clap their hands." (Isaiah 55:12) The Psalmist speaks of that time saying, "Then shall all the trees of the wood sing for joy before the Lord; for He comes to judge and govern the earth!" I believe that every fall, as God paints His singing hills, He is anticipating that grand, gala denouement of Christ's coming to judge and govern the earth—and saying "Rejoice!"

Fall is also a time of "putting by" the harvest in jars, freezers or root cellars in preparation for winter. It is the time for the final cutting and stacking of wood, cleaning the chimneys, mulching the gardens and making other provisions for the coming winter. So Fall speaks to me symbolically, of preparations of hearts and lives for the "winter" of "holy history."

Winter does come to the canvas. It is a time of great beauty combined with great hardship. Where my garden grew—there is death. My bright annuals are gone forever, but my perennials, though sleeping, will "rise again" next spring. The brilliant leaves of last season are now brown and dead—their work is over. Yet, composting, they will enrich the life of another season. The sap in the bare, bereft trees on our ridge will also rise, when spring comes and new leaves will form. There is death, yet there is hope.

Winter is the darkest, most severe season of them all—it is the death of the "old order." I see in winter the symbol of the time of judgment on the earth, when earth reaps what it has sown, and the darkness and severity of Great Tribulation envelop the globe.

But in the midst of the darkness and severity of winter here in New Hampshire, Burt and I travel through snow-ladened hills to a little white, New England church and with others, lift our voices and proclaim, "Joy to the world, the Lord is come, let earth receive her King!" The carols and celebration of the coming of the Lord interrupts and brings joy in the midst of the coldest winter. And as Christ came to Bethlehem to bring light to sin's darkness and to find and to redeem His own, so He promises to come again, when the darkness of Tribulation lies heavy on the earth. In power, in majesty and in great glory He will come, and "every eye will see Him." Then, in triumph, He will usher in His New Order, His glorious Reign, His Eternal "Spring!"

As I contemplate these ideas and images, and as I share with you further thoughts grown here in New England, it is my prayer that we, God's people, may be alert to where we may be on His cosmic calendar, and that with fervent dedication we all might echo Christ's own words,

"I must work the works of him that sent me, while
it is day; the night cometh, when no man can work."

(John 9:4)

ROW BY ROW

Snow Melting Time

The March sun is warm and the snows are subsiding. I hear the sweet sounds of that assurance as the melting snow drips continually from my roof. The garden and pasture fencing is even coming into sight. Here in New Hampshire we grow *fences* in March!

Other things are emerging also as the snow recedes— numerous cat food dishes which dog, Ben, confiscated and buried over the winter, along with various objects and papers he "tastefully" selected out of the garbage for chewing and romping. Coming to light also are assorted items we humans have dropped, or which winter winds have transported and relocated. Too, there are dirty layers of black soot from the huffing and puffing of our woodstoves. All this dirt and debris is showing itself as the melting snow withdraws before the warmth of approaching spring.

This doesn't make for the most attractive landscape— but it is most welcome. It brings us hope for the verdant seasons and gives us opportunity to tidy-up the lawn and garden areas before the new shoots of spring emerge.

This revelation of winter's hidden, lost, and dirty things is gradual—beginning first on the south side of the house and hill, and finishing, finally, in the deep woods where winter's cold vestiges linger, even while daffodils bloom in bright exhilaration in the garden beds.

So it is in us. As the Son's action—through the Light of His love, the Word, and the Spirit, gradually warms our inmost being, from the most obvious areas to the deep woods of our inner thoughts, debris is revealed, long covered by layers of time. Hidden, lost, and dirty things come to light—not to condemn us, but simply to assure us of verdant seasons to follow, and afford us the occasion to tidy up the landscape of our lives in preparation for His Spring.

Lord, thank You for Your warmth. Give me grace not to resist the exposure of unattractive attitudes and actions long buried within me. But may I welcome such revelation as opportunity, through Your cleansing, for a clearer heart wherein Your new plantings may thrive.

In Jesus' Name.

Lost Freshness

Winter is going, and I'm glad. The snow, once soft and welcoming, is now icy, crusty, and hard from repeated thawing and refreezing. My path today was unsure, even dangerous, for as I walked—or rather, attempted to walk—in the woods on what appeared to be firm footing, I suddenly and often sank knee-deep and thigh-deep through the unstable icy crust. I slipped wildly, like some cartoon character, on patches of slick ice and hit it hard. This activity is not recommended for maximum health benefit!

But only a few weeks back, the snow was soft, powdery, glistening—inviting show-shoers, skiers, and appreciative beauty-beholders. Now—its freshness is lost.

Earth seems to have a way of spoiling freshness—making things stale, hard and crusty—from snows to strudel; from heavenly manna of the wilderness times, which molded or melted when it stayed around too long, to our "well-preserved" bodies which, though oiled and greased by both "Ben Gay" and "Mary Kay" still kink and wrinkle up after they stay around awhile.

Freshness is a delicate, desirable quality, yet in our religious habits we seem to fear it, preferring, even demanding, the old methods, the safe old traditions—even if a smidgen stale, to taking a risk with the spontaneity of God. Sadly, in our religious doings, we really don't want to be *surprised*—even by the Holy Spirit of God.

But God desires freshness—"new mercies every morning," anointing us with "fresh oil," feeding the candlesticks of our churches with that continual supply of golden oil through the golden pipes from the olive trees spoken of in Zechariah's prophecy. God desires to give us an ample supply but not to have us package it, can or dry it, to store it for use at some distant time or place. That would eliminate our need for frequent visits to the Throne. But He desires to have us come to Him often—hourly, even moment by moment—not only to receive our provisions, but just to be there with Him, enjoying His company!

So the fear of the fresh must go, if God's manna is to be fresh. The oil of the Holy Spirit must be continual in our experience, or else our experience in Christ will become stale, hard, and crusty—even dangerous to our walk.

> *Forgive us, Lord, for being afraid of You—Your spontaneity and surprises. Help us know that what You do is always consistent with Who You are. Teach us, that it is not by the might of our stored wisdom, not by the power of our past successes, but only by the continual supply of Your Holy Spirit that we can accomplish anything of eternal value.*
>
> *In Jesus' Powerful Name.*
> *Amen.*

"Not by might, nor by power, but by My Spirit, saith the Lord of Hosts." (Zechariah 4:6)

"To everything there is a season . . ."
Ecclesiastes 3:1

It is "mud season" in New Hampshire! Oh dear! I am sure there is not one resident of the State who, daily, even hourly, is not wishing it would end. But then comes "black fly season"—and that one, also lingers too long in anybody's book. Oh, the impatience of waiting for the hard seasons to pass and the pleasant ones to arrive! This is true not only physically, but it seems even harder, spiritually, to wait for the "due season" when we will "reap if we faint not" (Galatians 6:9). It is extremely hard not to faint before fulfillment; intensely frustrating to wait when we would proceed. One of the tightest reins on our spirits is "Wait, wait, wait. . ."

But Song of Solomon gives a beautiful example of this discipline. The chosen Bride is compared by her Beloved to "a company of horses in Pharoah's chariots" (Song of Solomon 1:9). Now, offhand, one might not consider being compared to a horse as all that complimentary! However, Pharoah's white horses were something else! Exquisitely groomed and decorated, their muscles rippling with vital energies, they were totally under the control and exacting discipline of their master. Their exuberant desires and strengths were held in check until his moment of release, his "season" of motion. If they were to convey the king, they had to wait *properly* for the master's signal, waiting with expectancy and readiness, yet without restlessness or motion until the time was right.

Likewise, we who would convey the King to our generation, must learn to wait properly for our Master's perfect timing, His "seasons" for releasing us to action, and in fulfilling His promises to us. We may be tempted to give up hope, yet Hebrews 3:14 warns, "we share in Christ, if only we hold our first confidence firm to the end." We may be tempted to complain, to be restless and to doubt. Yet wavering unbelief is dangerous, and may cause us to forfeit the promise. As James instructs us in his epistle, we are to ". . .ask in faith, nothing wavering. For he that wavereth is like a wave of the sea driven with the wind and tossed. . .let not that man think that he shall receive anything from the Lord." (James 1:7) Also, we have the frightening account of the Israelites, whose dead bodies were strewn in the wilderness, for "the message which they heard did not benefit them, because it did not meet with faith in the hearers." (Hebrews 4:2 RSV)

So we must wait with expectancy, with the "sure hope" of the faithfulness of God, confidently declaring, "hath he said, and shall he not do it? or hath he spoken, and shall he not make it good?" (Numbers 23:19)

This is faith. And such faith maintained over the long haul, is patience—necessary as well. As Hebrews 6:12 encourages us, "be. . .followers of them who through faith and patience inherit the promises."

Also, we must wait with joy, "rejoicing in hope;" we must wait with peace, as the Psalmist expressed, "my flesh shall rest in hope." (Psalm 16:8) And we must wait with persistence, continuing to praise God for His promises. As the prophet Isaiah enjoins us, "You who are his servants and by your prayers put the Lord in remembrance of His promises, keep not silence, give Him no rest until He establishes Jerusalem and makes it a praise in the earth." (Isaiah 62:6-7 AMP.)

So here in New Hampshire in the spring, although I may grumble at the mud, I know, confidently, that this season will end, and more pleasant ones will follow. But I hope to learn not to grumble at the waiting times of God, for surely, if I "faint not," His promises will be fulfilled in His season.

Lord, help me to wait properly. Thank You that You have promised, and You will perform it.

In Jesus' Name.

"What's new? What's new?"

•

Strange, our fascination with the new. One seldom hears "What's old? What's old" (Except in places like New Hampshire where "old" means "antique and valuable" or "tried and true," and "new" is just a little suspect.) But here, in Spring, even perhaps more than many other places, the "new" is most welcome. The cold is old; the heavy clothing seems to have gained a few pounds over the winter; even the snow which was so "virgin" now has marks of man and machine, and we find ourselves looking more for swelling buds than for snowflakes.

But the enormous preoccupation with what's new in the world still does seem a bit warped. How many events get prime-time coverage on the "NEWS" or publicized in black and white press, just because they happened recently, not because they are of particular merit? In fact, the media skies can get so clouded with flocks of starlings, that one would hardly notice a bluebird.

Realistically, isn't it more important by far, to know what is *true* than what is *new*.

> *Time* magazine expounds
> Contemporary thought
> To keep us up with what's around—
> Desirous vantage sought.
> But better that we know
> Events transpiring where
> The greater *Time* is published—
> To know what's up, up there!

22

This desire *to know*, be it information of little consequence, or substantial eternal verities—this quest of knowledge has been both man's downfall and his salvation. It is what got us into all the trouble in Eden, and it also is what opens the gate for the return to Paradise. To seek to know, for pride's sake leads to doom, but to seek to know the Lord is life eternal.

How gracious, yet how dangerous of God to implant in man not only the mechanisms of learning, but the desire to discover. Seeking and finding has been the adventure of toddlers emptying mothers' purses, to astronauts exploring space. Seeking is even commanded—"Seek ye the Lord while he may be found." (Isaiah 55:6) and crowned with the pinnacle promise of Jeremiah 29:13-14, "And ye shall seek me, and find me, when ye shall search for me with all your heart, and I will be found of you, saith the Lord."

To seek to know Him and to know His ways should consume our hearts, as it did the heart of Paul. We hear him speak the depths of his desire, "that I may know him . . ." (Philippians 3:10) and we observe in Moses, a man "whom the Lord knew face to face" (Deuteronomy 34:10) and made known to him "his ways" at a time when the Israelites were only allowed to see "his acts." (Psalm 103:7) How paltry to be only an observer of acts, when we may know His ways.

Yet for this there is a price—a separating of ourselves unto Him, and from all that would detract, all that would keep us from "single" vision. Even knowledge itself, when its content is not in accord with the lessons God is trying to teach us at that particular time, may hinder His work, by distracting us from His choice of curriculum.

23

Too much banal information assimilated, too much discussion of trite topics—even good "religious" topics, can dilute the "concentration" of truth upon which God would have us meditate at that time.

I found it so. When a desire for "a single eye" became strong, then the promised "light" of the Lord revealed pockets of pride in some of my motivation "to know"— for instance, I did not want to *appear* "uninformed" on world events or current articles in Christian magazines. Although I was interested in these things, I was embarrassed if I did not know—to the point where, before dinner dates with people whose approval mattered, I would crash course *Time* magazine, *Eternity, Christianity Today*, cramming like a college kid for an exam—just so as not to be embarrassed by being ignorant. Not to tont ignorance as a virtue—but the need for approval, and attempting to be approved by what I knew was insecurity, inappropriate to a child of God. And having an "image" to maintain was self, and pride, also inappropriate.

So, when I heard, "Come away, my Beloved," I came. And I still need to come, for we do not easily overcome temptations to distraction. It is not a matter, necessarily, of "heading for the hills"—although we did that. But even here in the hills, the temptation lurks—to listen so much to earthly noise, that the "still, small voice" can scarcely be heard.

> Distance lends perspective—
> Wilderness, a post
> Where truth, of God's elective,
> May speak without a host
> Of man's interpretations—
> Like layers of veneer

24

Or varnishes on paintings rend
Original, less clear.

Help me, God, to be still—to hear and to know
You.

In Jesus' Name.

Community Christian Academy

Tucked among our New Hampshire hills, snugly settled beside the river called "Contoocook," stands an old, white New England farmhouse. Here an early family farmed the lush river valley, planting their seeds, row by row. Here, their frisky animals grazed in the bright green pasture, drank from the cool river, and were protected from the dark and cold in the old barn adjoining the house.

Now, the farmhouse and barn are "converted" into a Christian elementary school called "Community Christian Academy." The bright, cheery rooms of the old home now house bright, cheery children and in this place, seeds of truth are being planted and are flourishing.

It is spring, and the children who have been protected here from the winter cold, now stand in rows, waiting to go out to frolic in the green playground, "like calves released from the stalls."

They are precious, blessed children, and we of the School Board are blessed as we look on and see what God is doing in these little lives.

Looking on, it occurs to me that this little school, this Community Christian Academy is, in a sense, a microcosm, a small symbol of that Greater Community Christian Academy—that ageless, world-wide training school in which God educates His children—*all* of us, His frisky kids. *That* School, He has set among His protective "everlasting hills," established beside the everflowing

River of His Spirit, in the spiritually "converted" structure of our being and where once only "natural" crops grew, now eternal seeds and plantings of His supernatural grace are flourishing.

Part of God's job description is teaching the kids. And He is the Master-Teacher! He plans our schedules, orders our lessons, insisting that we repeat them again and again when we do poorly, or fail. He does this with all the kindness and patience that only God doesn't run out of!

But in many ways, this Greater Community Christian Academy is *very* different from *any* school we have *ever* attended! Some of its distinctives are:

1. It is a very "Private" school—run only for the family of the Master-Teacher. However, the general public is invited to join the family!
2. Although it is a "Royal" school, contemporary society does not consider it to have much "class."
3. It is a *very* expensive school—requiring all you have and are.
4. There is only *one* textbook. It's called *"The Book."*
5. In this school, it is all right to "worship" the Teacher—in fact, He insists on it!
6. It is also all right to bring "fruit" to the Teacher. He even requires it, calling it the "fruit of the Spirit"—things like love, joy and peace.
7. Here, one must never look *down* on a "lower classman." Actually, you never know exactly what grade you are in, yourself—in fact, you are probably in several different grades in different subjects all at the same time. Now no one but God could keep all *those* records straight, and He

doesn't show anyone the record book—at least, not yet!

8. In this school, there is a *lot* of "homework," but you never have to go off to your room alone to work it out. The Teacher always goes with you, offering His help.

9. Exams are never pre-announced—particularly, the "Final!"

10. Sharing answers during "testing times" is not only allowed, it is encouraged. As a matter of fact, here, "cheating" means *not* helping your fellow student when he is being tested!

11. Here, even the Teacher whispers help to you during "testing times."

12. According to the rules, there is to be no "competition" between students in this school, no comparing one student with another. They explain,

"In Christian education
You get what *you* deserve—
The Master-Teacher does not
grade you on the curve!"

13. Even when you *pass* an exam, you may be sure you will be re-tested on the same material periodically.

14. There are no vacations—not even any weekends off from school rules. But there is continual peace for students who do well.

15. There are no intramural, competitive sports—no separate teams to pit their strength against one another, no intramural debating teams to argue with one another. There is no squabbling allowed at all!

16. Rather, the "opposing team" is from the "outside." But they don't want to *play*, they really want to eliminate you!

17. So the athletic program is conducted for personal "fitness" and for "prayer-power" against evil.

18. There is *no* R.O.T.C. here, for *no* one is "on reserve."

19. No one gets away with *anything* here. The Master-Teacher knows *everything* that goes on, and He even says He plans to *post* it all some day and make it public!

20. The Master-Teacher is not afraid to discipline. In fact, He has a course He calls "Suffering," which they claim is very valuable.

21. The Master-Teacher has an extremely poor memory about some things. In fact, He *totally forgets* infractions of the rules when guilty students apologize. He calls it "repenting."

22. Every student's lessons are different, and no one is expected to know *everything* about *anything*. They say that complete knowledge is future, and often students are taught only one facet of a truth which needs to be combined with other facets taught to other students, before the "whole" can be seen. Therefore, students are not to criticize others' answers, as long as they are found in The Book, for even "right" answers may need to be combined in order to achieve what the Teacher calls "balance."

23. The whole student body will have to live together forever, and that's why the Teacher insists on cooperation now.

24. It is why He makes "Harmony" a required course.

25. In this school there is constant field work and "on-the-job" training. The Teacher says that mere "head knowledge" of the Text—without putting it into practice—can even kill the purpose of the whole thing, and that means *very* bad grades!

26. The Master-Teacher plans one big "Class-Day" (at that time there will be no "night") at which time He will give out awards. Those who have "finished the course" early still have to wait for everybody else, before getting their awards.

27. Trophies and prizes given to achievers will not be placed on their shelves or hung on their walls. They will be given right back to the Master-Teacher, even "laid at His feet" as the Book says.

28. Graduates will definitely not wear *black* regalia! Instead, they will walk around in *white!*

29. And—when it's all over—the Teacher is going to blow up the whole classroom! It has been hard for Him, too!

Steve's Commencement

Spring is Commencement time in Academia. Although Burt and I have been away from our teaching professions for awhile, and have traded our black regalia in for barn boots and "goat coats," still, Academia and its ways linger within us. Such as now—Commencement—time of "beginning." It is called that, but it surely *feels* more like an "ending." It takes more objectivity than I am capable of, to identify this termination of treasured times and friendships as a festive "beginning." But of course, it is. It is a time of great pomp and ceremony. . .

Commencement Procession

As dignified as Heads of State—Academicians in parades—
Regalias' satin stripes relate
Scholastic levels—(state of heads!)

Yet for all its dignity and celebration, for such as I, this disengagement of lives, closely woven together over past years, feels like a painful tearing of the texture. Always, at the many graduations at The Stony Brook School where I taught for a dozen years, there were tears galore when saying "good-bye" to cherished people.

But the most poignant commencement I remember occurred in 1981 at Gordon College, Wenham, Massachusetts, at our son, Stephen's graduation. Amid hundreds of friends and families, the Senior Class, clad in their handsome black regalia, sat together on the sunny soc-

31

cer field for the Commencement address. Each senior held a secret under his or her robe—an inflated, helium-filled balloon. Suddenly, at a signal and with loud shouts, a mass of bobbing, energetic, blue and white balloons were released. Caught quickly by the brisk north shore breezes, the balloons filled the sky, were wafted aloft and rapidly blew in all directions. As we watched them separate, taking their individual paths in pursuit of personal balloon destinies, they seemed to illustrate graphically the drama of this moment and of these lives now celebrating their parting. These close-clustered, "blue- and-white" Gordon College seniors whose lives would never reconvene, were about to be separated, taken by the winds in all directions in pursuit of their personal destinies.

The pain of such a parting, such a tearing, was very real. As Emily Dickinson expressed, "Parting is all we know of heaven—And all we need of hell."

And yet, there was celebration due, and festive excitement about it all. Personal destinies, adventures, fresh winds of opportunities were about to be experienced, and we all clapped and shouted with the Seniors.

Yes, "Commencement" is a good word, a proper word—positive, expectant, and full of forward faith. And God would give us a sense of those qualities, a personal commencement celebration every morning of the world. For no matter what pain and partings may accompany the day, His mercies, His compassions are "new every morning." Great is His faithfulness! His sun rises fresh and bright every morning, bursting in our windows to announce a new day, a new beginning.

So—let the balloons fly! It's Commencement time!

Roto-Tiller Time

It's roto-tiller time! We're ready for the kick-off for this year's garden game—the "Salad Bowl!" Burt pulls the cord, the roto-tiller roars into action and the garden cultivation is under way. Burt bought this roto-tiller soon after we came to New Hampshire, when he realized how vigorously the earth resists our efforts to "subdue" it— particularly the rocky soil of New Hampshire.

The tiller does good work, breaking up and preparing the soil for planting. We did not need such heavy equipment back on Long Island. Our gardens there were very meager, but here, we mean business! We're after a big harvest and we need all the help which power-equipment can give us.

God, too, is after a harvest. The curse on the earth makes the spiritual soil in hearts resistant, and His laborers in the field need all the help "power-equipment" can give. So God equipped the early church with "power tools," and told them to wait in Jerusalem to get them; told them not to try to do the job without them. How illogical for any who would labor in God's fields, to reject or ignore the Holy Spirit's anointing and power gifts, considering them unnecessary or even dangerous.

Our roto-tiller came with a book of instructions. Although it is a powerful tool, it is safe when Burt follows the book's directions. Likewise, the Book's instructions concerning the Holy Spirit's gifts must be obeyed for effectiveness and for safety's sake.

33

We use, but we do not "glorify" the roto-tiller. When guests have eaten tasty vegetables in our home, we do not gather in the equipment shed to praise the tiller. Rather, our guests thank us, the gardeners, for the food they have eaten. As with the Holy Spirit's gifts—they are not to be glorified, but rather, used, that the spiritual gardens of God might thrive, that He might have His desired harvest.

Lord, help us to be open to receive all the help You would give us! Fill us with Your Spirit. Anoint us with His power. Supply us with all the gifts necessary to do Your will with maximum effectiveness. Please.

For Your glory, and in Your Name.
Amen

That's the Chance He Takes!

God is heavily into gardens! According to the Book, He could hardly wait to plant one, and then, immediately, He got Adam involved in the project. He knew how good gardens are for men—in ways beyond meeting hunger pangs or even aesthetic needs. He knew that gardens give earthlings a wee glimpse of what it is like to be God—in planning and arranging living things in patterns and places for maximum productivity; how it feels to tend them, providing nutrients, light, water, cultivation and weeding; how it feels to have to take drastic measures sometimes, like pruning, thinning, transplanting, pinching back—hard things for a plant to cope with. And then, how it is to have to leave a great deal to the plants themselves—the assimilating of the nutrients and water, and the stretching toward the light in order to produce that of which they are capable, according to the pattern and life within them.

Gardener God did all that, and does all that for us. In the Song of Solomon He calls us His "garden." But the astonishing difference in God's garden of people, and in our gardens of peas and petunias, is that He took the wild risk of giving His plantings *free will!* He even lets His plants decide—in the first place—if they even *want* to be planted in His garden, or not. He then allows them to choose if they will assimilate His nourishings, absorb His waterings, orient and grow toward His light. He leaves it to their option if they will receive or reject His

tendings; if they will grow, or go to seed; if they will
fulfill their potential, or wilt without produce.

Could anyone hope to succeed with such a garden?

I guess that's the chance God takes!

"Eating Out"

What camaraderie with my grazing animals I feel this morning! As I work in the garden I can not resist nibbling on leaves of dew-washed lettuce, tiny sweet beans, tangy dill and other delicacies fresh from the earth. I am truly "dining out." The flavors are wonderful and I never cease to be amazed at how seeds planted in the same earth, receiving the same nutrients and waterings, end up with such a variety of distinctive flavors.

Flavor is certainly at its peak in summer, and our garden-fresh fruits and vegetables are a continual reason for praise—particularly when we can eat them outside—whether "eating out" in the garden, on the front porch, or in a favorite picnic setting. Somehow, outside, we feel closer to the Source of it all.

I wonder if, when the Source-of-it-all ate with His disciples, they ever thought to ask Him how He did it, how He came up with all those different flavors. I wonder if Christ ever talked recipes with Martha?

He certainly staged the largest picnics on record! Did you ever think of other ways He might have done it, instead of starting with paltry loaves and fish? He could have merely spoken a word, and the hunger of thousands could have simply disappeared! Or, angels with trays of succulent cuisine, might have passed among the crowd—or even food-bearing ravens, just for old times' sake.

But no, He chose to use a humble offering of loaves and fish, submitted by a child—to break, to bless, and to distribute to meet the needs of the multitudes.

Which He still does. Although capable of doing it in more striking, spectacular ways, He still chooses to receive the humble offerings of our lives and whatever comprises our "loaves and fish"—to break them—to bless them—and to send them forth, that the needs of multitudes might be met.

Thank you, Lord, for every delicious, distinctive flavor of Your earth. I offer to You my life this day, that with Your touch and blessing, those who partake may be blessed.

In Jesus' Name.

5 + 2

Loaves and Fish—
    not much of a dish—
But when, to God consigning—
One finds that there
    is food to spare,
For outdoor, "Pleasure Dining!"

Time—Friend or Foe?

It is summer here on the farm and there is so much to do, I honestly do not know where to begin. The old lyrics which describe "Summertime" as "when the living is easy. . ." were not written about a New Hampshire farm! True, there is no snow to shovel (usually) but in addition to our "normal" schedule of activities—church, family, real estate, art, etc., there is garden maintenance and processing of our wonderful fresh produce as it comes in season. Burt brings in baskets—even wheelbarrows full of vegetables, ready to be frozen, canned, or buried in sand or sawdust in the root cellar, and although the summer days are long, they are never long enough. I tend to overdo, and with weariness comes frustrations with the limitations of time and human energy. Frequently I need the reminder from the Psalmist about "today"—Whose it is—and what I'm to do in it. "This is the day which the Lord has made; let us rejoice and be glad in it." (Psalm 118:24)

Basically, this "today" which is His, is a reality only because of the system which God devised and called "time." Founded on His consistent, dependable natural laws, it assures me that today will have a predictable, specific beginning, as well as a reliable, split-second ending. Today will not be *late*, either coming or going—although *I* probably will be—for something or other; but not because I want to be contrary. I simply find it difficult to bow to and to adapt my doings to that impersonal tyrant called "Time."

This prejudice against Time is of long standing, and as most prejudices, doesn't hold up under scrutiny and analysis. Time is, in truth, our benefactor, keeping the world's watches synchronized and the T.V. shows coming on when they say they will be there. (As if we had time to watch them!) But Time does lend a certain measure of security and predictability to this insecure and spinning earth. For that I am grateful.

But I still don't wear watches—at least not any that run. Burt's parents gave me Grandmother Lauber's lovely gold locket watch, which they had repaired and put in running order for me—but I honestly can't remember to wind it. The few clocks around the house and in the car, and Burt's honking in the driveway usually get me where I'm supposed to be at least close to the proper time. But there is something about wearing a watch that makes me feel handcuffed to my captor, and under pressure to march to his ticking.

I expressed this quarrel with Time a few years ago in these lines:

> Free of earth's bridles
> We would gallop
> Over laughing hills,
> Silly with wildflowers—
> Even through cotton candy clouds
> (Like Pegasus)—
> Manes tossing,
> Nostrils filling
> With fragrant winds.
> But Time
> Is a Harness—

Tight,
Restricting—
Confined to our circles,
We trot our circuits—
Breathing dust.

Now, thanks to God and His Holy Spirit's refreshing, I no longer breathe "dust," but instead have caught the scent of those fragrant winds which flow among the "laughing hills." I still experience frustration when Time and I find ourselves at loggerheads, and I find myself far behind in what needs doing, but I may have a handle on my problem; at least I understand it more clearly.

Some early Greeks helped me out. They apparently had similar struggles, so they did a little chop-chop on the word "time." They divided it into two words: the first, "chronos" which means the "system" regulating and organizing all those charts and clocks which keep the world synchronized; and secondly, "kairos" or "season"—the "reason," the purpose and meaning which fills any prescribed span of "chronos." Thus, "chronos" is the structure; "kairos," the content. Structure without content is cold, heartless and empty—like a house without occupants. But occupants need houses; so "kairos" needs "chronos." Chronos provides the order, or container, to hold kairos, the content. Chronos serves like a bowl, to keep the fruit from rolling off the table.

So Time is, after all, a good system—a friend, not a foe. God made it "and saw that it was good," and I ought not argue with that. God made "today" with its chronos ("This is the day which the Lord has made") and I am to participate in its kairos ("let us rejoice and be glad in it.")

So I must make friends with Chronos (I've always loved Kairos!) knowing that he is my servant and not my tyrant. He tries his best to keep my life from getting jumbled, and I am the culprit, not he, when things get tangled. For when my "flesh" is not totally harnessed by the Spirit, I attempt to force more "content" into a time "container" than will fit, and it all spills over and makes a mess.

Another problem, perhaps for all of us, is the concept of time being "ours." That makes us possessive, and irritable when we are interrupted. By contrast, there is peace in the knowledge that my days are God's gift to me, and my gift back to Him. That gives me freedom to "spend" time under His direction, in ways that may not seem "practical" to man. It affords the freedom to "give" time, under His leading and to welcome without resentment those who would "take" time, when He has sent them.

But the knowledge that my time belongs to Him carries responsibility as well. I dare not "waste" it. I must reverence its moments, guard its purposes and cherish its opportunities. I must reverence as well, the time of others, knowing that it, too, is precious.

Lord, help me to follow Your Spirit's leading; thus to walk in freedom—knowing that as I move to Your cadence, dancing and rejoicing will fill this day which You have made.

In Jesus' Name.

"God took him." Or did He?

My lovely flowers blooming so beautifully today in my
summer garden will die in a few weeks. The bright
yellows of my marigolds, the deep pinks and reds of my
petunias, the rich blues of my delphinium will all be
brown after the first frost arrives. I expect that. And
although they have given to me their beauty, and I have
given to them my care and appreciation, when their
season is over, I accept their death, pull them out or
mulch them over, and then look forward to spring.

But today I am disturbed. My nasturtiums are dead.
Only a day or so ago they were as vivid as any flower
could be, but today they are withered and gone. It is only
July and they should have had several more weeks of
blooming, but they died prematurely when they were at-
tacked by insect enemies. I was not alert enough and did
not see the problem in time to spray and save them.
Nature did not "will" their death at this time, but according to the rules of the contest, the bugs won.

Now I wonder if there is a correspondence here, in
how God's will relates to human life and death matters—
at least a shade of similarity? God certainly desires life,
liberty and happiness for all mankind—or else Jesus
would not have died to make those things possible. But
the free-will clause in the charter of creation leaves open
options and alternatives. God set the rules—and He, and

we, and the enemy (Satan and his cohorts—the "bugs") play by those rules. If by reason of ignorance or apathy, sin or lack of spiritual power, we give away our protection and victory, the "bugs" *could* win.

As with the Israelites. God ordained victory for them. He *gave* them the land. But they either *took* the land, or they failed in the conquest according to their obedience, their adherence to His rules. In fact we are told that God deliberately left some enemies in the land so that the young Israelites might learn war, and for testing to see "whether Israel would obey the commandments of the Lord." The test could go either way, depending on the attitudes and actions of Israel. (Judges 3:1-4)

But could this optional clause extend so far as death? Scripture says it does. Moses laid it out straight. "I have set before you life and death, blessing and curse; therefore choose life, that you and your descendants may live, loving the Lord your God, obeying His voice, and cleaving to Him; for that means life to you and length of days. . ." (Deuteronomy 30:19-20 RSV)

But that's Old Testament. What about the era of grace? Could New Testament Christians really die without it being the will of God? We are told that some did—in Corinth, because they partook "unworthily" of the Lord's Supper—"that is why many of you are weak and ill, and some have died." (I Corinthians 11:30 RSV) There are a number of such scary Scriptures, such as I Corinthians 3:17—"If any man defile the temple of God, him shall God destroy; for the temple of God is holy, which temple ye are." It sounds an awful lot like reaping what one sows.

But what about good people, those who have sown

45

good? What about Dorcas? In the midst of all her doing good, she up and died—but her friends wouldn't hear of it! They got Peter on the job, and sure enough, she came back to life. Surely God would not have raised her from the dead, even at the request of Peter, had it been His will for her to die—at least to stay dead. Certainly Jesus would not have countered His Father's will by raising people to life whom the Father willed dead. Jesus was not a show-off; He did His Father's will perfectly. He healed all who came to Him; He raised several from the dead

And beyond that, He commanded His disciples, "Heal the sick, raise the dead. . ." among other things. (Matthew 10:8) "Yes," I have said, "but that was back then." However, one day it hit me that the Great Commission (Matthew 28:19-20) which I recited innumerable times as the motto verse for the "Girls' Auxiliary" back in the First Baptist Church of Jackson, Mississippi, contained these words, ". . .teaching them to observe all things whatsoever I have commanded you. . ." Did He really mean that "all" the things He had commanded *them* to do, were to be expected of *us* as well? Could that mean healing the sick, raising the dead?

If those who were to come to Christ through the preaching of the gospel were to be taught to practice *all* the commands of Christ to the apostles, why have we not been taught about healing the sick and raising the dead? Have we been hoodwinked into assuming, fatalistically, that *all* illness is to be endured patiently for the good lessons it teaches, and that *every* death is according to the will of God, and to be accepted without question or prayer?

Perhaps we have. Perhaps we should look afresh at the healed bodies and empty tombs of the New Testament and see if we have allowed the enemy—the "robber," the "murderer from the beginning," to rob the health and snatch away through death, some whom the Lord would have restored had we been more attuned to His ways, more empowered by His might; if we have allowed some to be taken away prematurely, like my nasturtiums, when they should have had longer to bloom.

Forgive us, Lord, if we have confused fatalism with faith; if, even though we know You can *do the impossible, we have doubted that You* would. *Forgive us, if we have allowed the "bugs" to win.*

In Jesus' Name.

47

Lucy's Lesson

". . . because of his shameless persistence and insistence, he will get up and give him as much as he needs. So I say to you, Ask and keep on asking, and it shall be given you; seek and keep on seeking, and you shall find; knock and keep on knocking, and the door shall be opened to you."

(Luke 11: 8,9 AMP)

Lucy is a cat—one of her mother, Katrina's, first litter. Her presence in this home is clear evidence of modern-day miracles, for Burt offered (without so much as a subtle request from me) to let me keep one of Katrina's first born. (A cat-lover, Burt is not!) But even a non-cat-lover could not help but at least *respect* Lucy. She is an extremely fluffy, dignified grey tiger, who carries her bushy fox-like tail straight up as she runs.

And Lucy is no dope. She's got *my* number. Also she knows that there is something more interesting, beyond normal cat food rations, in our refrigerator—and she is determined to have it. Periodically through the day she will arrive in the kitchen, post herself beside the refrigerator door, stare at me—and wait. She doesn't budge. She doesn't "meow" and complain. She just watches and waits, as long as it takes, and sooner or later, she is rewarded!

Now I feed all the cats well. They all get their "Kat-Krumbles," "Meow-Mix," "Dixie Dinner," and "Seafood

48

Platter." But Lucy knows there is something better; she knows where it is; she knows who will give it to her (she doesn''t pull this with Burt); and she has the importunity to wait until I open the door and dole out morsels of leftover chicken, ham, roast beef, or cheese.

However—I may be in big trouble. Through Lucy's example, Katrina and Bo Peep are beginning to catch on.

Lucy's lesson is obvious. God is kinder than I; He has more than scraps to give away; and He rewards the faith that keeps on asking, keeps on persevering—waiting with faith that recognizes the nature of the Giver, and confidence that knows His storehouse is full.

Thus, a fluffy grey tiger cat, named Lucy, illustrates for me,

> When praying, saying "Please"—and *leaving*,
> Results in limited receiving.
> Forget the fretting, quitting, fainting—
> Persevere with watchful waiting!

Help me, Lord, to persist in prayer, my eyes on You, knowing that door will open and I will receive from the abundance of Your table.
In Jesus' Name.

"They're Gone!"

Today was special—*very* special for some darling little barn swallows I have loved ever since they broke through their egg shells and poked their funny little heads over the rim of their nest, which their courageous mother perched on a rafter in our barn only a foot or so above our heads. Each day I have watched their growth, talked a little bird-talk with them, and laughed out loud at the comical appearance of their gigantic beaks and tufted heads. Daily through these past weeks we have visited, observing one another eye-ball to eye-ball, and I hope, somewhere in their bird consciousness, they have felt the warmth and blessing I have wished upon them.

They need blessing today, as well as in the days to come. This is the day we have watched for, in order to keep our cats inside, to reduce the risks the fledglings will face when first meeting the world head-on. We knew the day was near, for there was by far more bird than there was nest. As the chicks have grown, the nest has seemed to grow smaller, requiring "double-decker" sleeping. Each morning lately, as Burt has gone to the barn for early chores, I have waited to hear the inevitable announcement, "They're gone!"

Today I heard it. I secured the cats as protective-mother-instincts rose in me—along with sadness. (I get too "attached" to such creatures.) I wondered where they had gone, and if all four would return to the barn tonight, for they do come back to "sleep home" for a little while. I went to the front porch for morning devotions, and lo and behold—perched on the pasture fence right in front of me, were all four baby swallows, their faithful mother near-by, coaching their new maneuvers. I felt honored to attend their "coming-out" party! And I wondered what *they* were feeling . . .

First Day Out of the Nest

Perched atop my fence rail
    four in a row—
Fledgling barn swallows
    With *everywhere* to go!
From overcrowded quarters
    To wide expansive sky—
Tight wings, non-functional and cramped—
    Suddenly can fly!
Awesome blue mountains
    Surprise their baby eyes;
Their former dim, barn light
    Replaced by bulb the size
And wattage of June sunshine—
    What an astounding world!
I wonder what they're thinking
    After being hurled
Into *bird-boggling* splendor. . .

    Could similar delight

    Await the saints' sensation
        On our *Translation flight?*

". . . then we which are alive and remain shall be caught up . . . in the clouds, to meet the Lord in the air . . ." (I Thessalonians 4:17)

Thank you, Lord, for that glorious prospect! What a flight that will be!

In Jesus' Name.

And, P.S. Please take care of my barn swallows.

Amen.

On Lions and Lambs

Our little white lambs, born this spring are frolicking in the green pasture among the yellow buttercups—a scene befitting a calendar photograph. The joy of watching these little creatures far outweighs the bleary, bleak "all-nighters" spent attending the mother ewes in complicated deliveries. I have yet to become accustomed to the 3:00 A.M. "barn-checks" which are necessary during lambing season, and we still have very much to learn about sheep mid-wifery!

The things which we have learned about sheep are not terribly complimentary to us who are called "the sheep of His pasture." Our sheep are nervous and fearful—and any animal afraid of *me* is dumb! They are witless enough to leap headlong into a fence, over which or through which there is not the slightest chance of making it. For the most part, they are reluctant to come to receive pats or hugs—unlike our goats, who eat it up—along with most anything else. The sheep usually bolt away from me, the one who cares for them, feeds them, hauls their water buckets, and helps deliver their young.

And yet with all their faults, they are valuable to us. We appreciate their beauty, we love the winsomeness of the lambs, but their greatest contribution is in their dying, and how they go about it. They bleat, and raise a rumpus when they hear the grain scoop, but they die quietly, without complaint. Meekly, they give themselves away in death.

"Behold the Lamb of God!" enjoined John the Baptist. The Lamb of God—the dying Lamb—willing to give Himself away quietly in death.

Is that quality of lambhood applicable to us, the "sheep of his pasture?" Are we like Christ, the Lamb of God, in that quality of willingness to lay down our lives? Not too often, I suspect. We do better with the *living* lamb symbol—the skittish, wandering, crashing into fences lamb—the dense, fearful lamb, reluctant to come to the one who loves it best, who holds nothing but good intent toward it, who desires to pat and hug it—*that* lamb we resemble more closely than the meek, dying lamb.

Somehow dying, giving ourselves away in self-denial, self-forgetfulness is not our strong suit, generally. We usually prefer to have our own way, assert our strong wills, even force others to comply, if possible. We're a bit closer to lions than lambs in our relationships with others.

But wait! Christ was called a "Lion"—the Lion of the tribe of Judah,"—the ruling king of the animal world symbolizing the ruling King of all worlds. Christ Jesus, the "Lion," ruled over darkness, sin and evil; He conquered the evil one and his deeds; He cast out demons; He commanded diseases to leave; and in that ultimate victory, He forced His will and His way over the powers of death and hell! What a Lion!

It seems to me that we've got it all backwards. For often we act like roaring *lions* toward one another—the "brethren" for whom we should be laying down our lives—and we act like fearful *lambs* toward the devil and his cohorts—the ones we should be addressing with the authority and rule of Jesus Christ. We *should* be "pulling down. . .strong holds. . .and every high thing that exalteth itself against the knowledge of God, and bringing into captivity every thought to the obedience of Christ." (II Cor. 10:4-5) We *should* be spiritually *violent*—in *prayer*—proclaiming the authority of Jesus' Name over evil, courageously using our spiritual weapons against spiritual wickedness in aggressive Spirit-led warfare, for "the violent take it by force." (Matt. 11:12)

Instead, we scurry in fear, leap into fences, and get ourselves "walloped." We're aggressive toward people, but wimps toward the devil! How desperately we need to follow our Lord, as He ruled triumphantly over evil, and died graciously for people.

The people of Revelation 12 combined both lion and lamb qualities: ". . .they overcame him (Satan) by the blood of the Lamb, and by the word of their testimony..." (They waged Lion-like war against the forces of evil through the power of the blood of Jesus, and through verbally attesting their faith in His victory.) ". . .for they loved not their lives unto the death." (Rev. 12:11) (They had the Lamb-like willingness to lay down their wills, their desires, and even their physical lives for Jesus' sake.)

What an example!

Lord, please help us get it straight. May we be both Lamb-like, and Lion-like—but toward the right folks!

In Jesus' Name.

Our Garden Maturing

"Grow up into Him in all things." (Ephesians 4:15)

Summer is the time for growth and maturing. Our spring lambs are gaining weight, and the new goat kids are romping with the older goats on the huge boulders in the pasture, playing "king of the mountain." The corn is now much taller than I, and I walk, completely hidden between the rows, feeling I am in a secret world of my own. Fat ears are forming on the corn stalks, ears which will soon be dripping in butter. Yet, in the rows next to the corn, the acorn squash is an immature yellow, and in the front field, the pumpkins are still green. All the vegetables mature at different times, and although we want all of them to "keep at it," keep on growing and developing, we are patient and do not chide the chard, acorn squash, or pumpkin because they are not ready for the table in August.

Now if the same God Who programmed vegetables, planned people as well, then it stands to reason that we, in the Body of Christ will not mature at the same rate in every area of our lives. We have more differences than do corn and broccoli and the God Who made us is patient. He commands us to "grow up," but our individual growth rates and seasons for maturing are to be found in His garden book alone. Just so long as we all "keep at it," encouraging one another, building one another up, "fainting not" when we become weary—then, the Lord of the Harvest can reap His due, can have His parent heart satisfied when finally He sees His kids all grown up, "all come in the unity of the faith, and of the knowledge of the Son of God, unto a perfect man, unto the measure of the stature of the fullness of Christ." (Ephesians 4:13)

Our Daughter Maturing

Our daughter Pamela is a lovely young lady, married and a mother. But when she was only nine months old, we gave her a large Teddy bear which she loved, cuddled and tossed around throughout her childhood. But now, with a husband to love and a little son to cuddle, dear Teddy Bear is relegated to the shelf—a silent, tender reminder of childhood days. He is not played with any more, for Pam has "put away childish things."

Would that we all "put away childish things" in matters of heart. How often we grown-up folks hold tenaciously to concepts and feelings we should have outgrown years ago. Somehow we resist change, yet growth demands change. How tragic if our children did not grow; how disappointing if our gardens did not mature; and how saddened God must be when His people refuse to put away Teddy Bear ideas and attitudes when it is time to grow up.

Pam's Teddy Bear sits on the shelf—
Discarded—in his spot—
As is the "image" he conveyed—
(A *real* bear, he is not!)
Pam's all grown-up, so now she knows
How big a *real* bear is—
Maturity transformed her thought—
The change was *hers*, not his!
Feel free, dear Lord, to shelve the lot

Of what I *think* I know—
Replace young concepts I may hold,
With grown-up *Truth* that's so!

Fall

I suppose that Fall is called "Fall" because the leaves fall down—but then, again, I could be wrong. Basically, it is an "up" season—breathtaking color, harvest, and *no bugs!* In New Hampshire *that* makes for "up"!

The summer people have closed their cottages, packed their campers, and have gone home, thinking they got the icing off the New Hampshire cake—the best of the seasons. But they didn't. In fact, they had just left when New Hampshire broke out in its most beautiful song! There simply are not words adequate to describe the color of the New England hillsides this time of year. When I paint them, my colors appear drab compared with the real thing. But after the season ends, and the earth returns to normal, my paintings look almost fake—as if nothing in a landscape could be that bright.

And the fragrances of fall are outstanding as well—the apples cooking on the stove, being made ready for jams or sauce; the smell of grapes on the arbor, full ripe; and the hint of wood smoke from old cook stoves as well as our new "Defiant"—all insist that one take many deep breaths.

And the warmth of these glorious Indian summer days, which one can soak in without sacrificing one's blood to the insect population, makes one wish the season would never end. God goes all out in decorating for this fall festival, with leaves brighter than any crepe paper, and sassy plump pumpkins and squash in "safety orange" and silly shapes. It is a festive time indeed.

It is what we have been after all year—the time of expectation fulfilled, of gathering that for which we have labored, of enjoying the rewards of faithful effort. That is reason to celebrate.

Fall always comes after spring and summer—physically and spiritually as well. That certainty brings both comfort and warning. We are comforted by knowing that at last, in "due season we will reap, if we faint not." But therein is the warning. Should we faint, give up, stop weeding, quit watering, let it go to seed—then no gala celebration or jolly pumpkin decorations shall be our due. For "if ye sow sparingly ye shall reap also sparingly." We will surely reap what we sow, for good or for bad, for celebration or for disappointment.

So then, may we keep at it, with courage, initiative and diligence. The fall season comes without fail, and is intended and designated on the calendar of God to be an "up" time of magnificent beauty and bounty.

"Cast not away therefore your confidence, which hath great recompense of reward. For ye have need of patience, that after ye have done the will of God, ye might receive the promise. For yet a little while, and he that shall come will come, and will not tarry."

(Hebrews 10:35-37)

Window-Washing Time

It's a magnificent fall day, and I'd rather be doing almost anything but washing windows. My good intentions tell me to wash them both spring and fall, but I must confess, my intentions are more accomplished than my accomplishments.

But I do get to it occasionally, and I'm at it today, making up silly jingles to amuse myself—"The pain of washing window panes, exceeds the normal household strains. . ."

It's not that I do not delight in sparkling, clean windows, but the tugging at these "easy-out" window sashes regularly breaks my fingernails, and the huge number of windows in our hilltop home makes this a monumental chore.

It seems that God took me literally when I penned this prayer a few years back:

> More windows in my house, Lord—
> Lord, build more windows in—
> Break through thick walls which I have built
> To shut "them" out, and shut "us" in.
> So renovate my house, to seem
> A "plaza" by comparison—
> That I be more concerned with light—
> And less, with "garrison."

He has answered that prayer both spiritually and

physically. For our home on Long Island was nestled and shaded in the woods, whereas our home here in New Hampshire is set high on an open hill, bright and sunny, with many guests coming and going—definitely more "plaza" than "garrison!"

All that makes for a lot of window washing. Today as I am about it, I am reminded of the diligence that is necessary if we are to keep our spiritual windows clean—the constant care required to keep the smudges, films and cobwebs from our hearts and lives. Both for His light to shine into us undimmed, and to shine from us with clarity and undiminished sparkle, we need unsmudged spiritual transparency.

That takes effort, just as does this ammonia water, paper-towel process I'm working at today. What is helpful, I find, is to stop periodically to look at the view—the view which is much clearer through the clean windows than the waiting ones. This renews my motivation—there is a view to be had! There is a vista to be enjoyed! There is purpose in all this!

Without purpose—defined and remembered—labor can become an end in itself, rather than the means to an end, and thus burdensome and wearing. The project, then, can distract from the purpose, can obscure the primary.

As in matters of the Spirit—our labors have purpose, our spiritual housecleaning has a goal—that we may see Him more clearly, and that His light may shine into and through us with greater purity and brilliance.

So my prayer today is:

that I may not be
So busy washing windows
That I fail to see the view—
Or so intent on serving, Lord,
That I lose sight of You!

In Jesus' Name.

"Coming! Ready or Not!"

It is true. Winter will come to our farm, whether we are ready for it or not. That word, "ready," has great significance here in the country in New England. It *can* be a quiet and comfortable word, reflecting the mood of nature as she settles down for a "long winter's nap." But only if one is prepared, if all the necessary chores are complete. Then, the word "ready" imparts a comfortable assurance, like a pat on the back, making one feel settled in his spirit, calmly sharing with nature—

> The silence grey November knows
> Quietly waiting for the snows.

Of course one dare not settle down if the chores of preparation are still waiting. (I still must mulch the garden, and our garage is half-filled with pumpkins and squash which need to be baked, mashed and frozen.) But Burt has the woodpiles filled in the wagon shed and on the front porch, ready and waiting for the cozy fires which will keep our tight log home toasty and comfortable all winter. So "ready?" stirs discomfort in me, whereas "ready" can speak assurance to Burt.

Now the same applies to readiness, in terms of being prepared for difficult times which many believe are approaching rapidly—in fact are already upon many throughout the world. If this is the fall season in "Heilig Geschichte"—holy history; if, according to God's calendar, we are approaching Judgment Winter, the death of the old order—are we ready? Are our hearts prepared? Have we stored and stacked in our being sufficient food and fuel of the Word of God? Do we have enough to share with others? Should Bibles and Christian literature become rare, have we hidden God's Truth in our hearts? Have we learned to depend on God in stress times *now*— "overcoming" rather than "undergoing?" Have we practiced rejoicing "always," giving thanks "in all things" to the point where, were human sources of pleasure removed, our cup of joy would still "be full?" Is our spiritual wiring in good repair—capable of maintaining light—even in case of an earthly "blackout?"

The "foolish virgins" of Matthew 25 were not so prepared—those gals waiting for the Bridegroom, who were "pure," whose only fault was the neglect of their "energy" supply. They missed something BIG!

Is the Holy Spirit oil *full* in our vessels? Are our lamps trimmed and ready? Scripture explains that it is God's Word that is a "lamp unto our feet." And with sufficient oil in their lamps, the "ready" virgins went in to the feast.

Are we prepared to burn brightly, to provide the light of witness to a darkened earth? Are we ready for winter?

Extreme?

"By faith Noah, being warned of God of things not seen as yet, moved with fear, prepared an ark to the saving of his house."

(Hebrews 11:7)

I do believe the leaves will soon be falling on the world. I believe we are on the brink of great revival, great ingathering, great harvest—that the winter season of earth's judgment is near, when unrighteousness shall be cleansed in preparation for the glorious springtime of Christ's reign on earth.

I believe that even now we are feeling the chilly winds of winter's warning in world economics, politics and nature, all early labor pains preceding the major distresses described in Matthew 24. Exact timing and details we are not to know; "the day and the hour knows no man" but we are to be alert to the signs of the season.

The Pharaohs of our day, the leaders in government, ecology, economics, politics are concurring that the world is in for it—that we are walking a tightrope with no safety net beneath us—that economic collapse, war, famine and total disaster are not "long shots" by a long shot. It is strange, how when they speak, they are taken seriously, but if a Christian states the same thing, he may be considered extreme, an alarmist, a "doom-and-gloomer."

"As in the Days of Noah. . ."

"Noah, is that what you say. . .
You think *the world will wash away?*

Though not to slander, or demean,
But aren't you *nuts?* at *least* extreme!"

But God did give the warnings to Pharaoh, and the in-
terpretation of the warnings to Joseph, His man. And as
a result, multitudes were provided for in the time of
disaster and God's Name was glorified.

May we, God's people, be sensitive to hear what the
Pharaohs are saying, and be sensitive to the Spirit of God,
to hear the meaning and the constructive preparations
to take. God told Noah what to do; God told Joseph how
to prepare—not just to save their own skins, but to be
used as His instruments of mercy and help to the world.
Had Noah been dense or afraid of ridicule and refused
to build his boat—the whole bunch of them would have
drowned and God would have had to start over from
scratch. Had Joseph been insensitive to the Spirit of
God—father Jacob and brother Judah would have starved
to death, and there goes the lineage of Jesus. It was important that they were able to hear, and willing to obey.

If then it is true, that we are approaching fall, symbol
of the period just prior to earth's judgment winter, may
we be sensitive to hear the instructions of the Spirit, and
do them. Spiritual preparation is first and foremost, certainly. But both Noah and Joseph were given outlines for
physical preparation as well. They were different from
one another, and surely, the Spirit of God will instruct

69

different people in different ways, according to His plan for their usefulness. He might want you to store food; He might ask you to relocate; you might need to learn food production; you might be required to depend on supernatural provision, so you had better learn faith now; you might need skills of a life-sustaining nature to support yourself and to help others, and now is the time to learn them. God alone knows—but surely if we are open, He will tell us.

Help us, God, to have ears to hear "what the Spirit is saying to the churches."
In Jesus' Name.

The Dead

". . .and the place thereof shall know it no more."

From the flower bed this morning, I pulled up my tall, dead cosmos, which only a few short days ago stood in stately, old-fashioned dignity, dressed in soft lilacs and pinks. Today, after the first freeze, they are brown, stiff, and very dead.

Impatience rose in me. I *had* to remove them quickly! "Why?" I pondered. "What's the hurry?"

"Because," my heart answered, "they are dead!" As annuals, they had seen their season, and now it is all over. Their beauty remains only in my memory, and even that remembrance is marred by the grotesque image of their dead forms.

We bury our dead. We treasure old photographs of the living whom we have loved, but when they die, we put away and cover their bodies. For with all the hope we have of resurrection, death is still painful and ugly—still the enemy, yet to be destroyed.

Scripture calls death our "servant." So I pull out my dead cosmos and pile them on the compost heap to serve me in another season, in another form.

But I do not make friends with death. It is hateful, despicable, the loathsome enemy who had robbed me of precious people whose love and lives are woven inextricably through my being. It has robbed me of dreams I have dreamed, and animals I have loved. And it is bent on my own destruction, as well.

So I have good reason to hurry to pull out of my garden the brown, blanched, withered and stiff remains of my flowers which shared their life and loveliness with me all summer. I want no reminder of death poking its head through the coming snow which will conceal and cover death's success. That pure, white covering will speak to me of Heaven's promise to make all things new—in that eternal day when LIFE will erase even the memory of my dead cosmos.

Thank you, Lord, for the sure hope of that day.

In Jesus' Name.

November Crossing *

On board the Cross Sound Ferry
En route to say "good-bye" to Dad
Before death comes.
Heartache and grief are crashing
Like waves against the ferry's hull—
This sea runs deep.
At Orient, I'll land soon.
The setting sun now stretches gold
Across the sea
As carpet, into harbor.

Lord, roll out the gold for Dad—
As path to port.
His hull is racked by waves of pain,
November crossing's turbulence—
Bone cancer's storm.
You, Lord—his life-long Orient—
His Harbor, Port—To You, Dad comes
On path of gold.

* On the Cross Sound Ferry, from New London, CT to Orient
Point, NY, November 7, 1985.

Crushed Grapes

"I am the vine, ye are the branches; He that abideth in me, and I in him, the same bringeth forth much fruit. . ."

(John 15:5)

"And he took the cup, and gave thanks, and gave it to them, saying, Drink ye all of it; For this is my blood of the new testament, which is shed for many for the remission of sins."

(Matthew 26:27- 28)

The grapes are ripe. The arbor which Burt built just outside my kitchen window stands adorned with luscious clusters of purple grapes, hanging on the green as Christmas tree ornaments.

Since I spend many hours a week here at my sink, I enjoy the view of the arbor and its reminder of Christ's symbol of Himself, the vine; and us, the branches. Today's kitchen project has inspired some new thoughts. I'm making grape jam. I am energetically crushing these gorgeous grapes to release their goodness. The good fruit which the branches took time and energies to produce, I am smashing into a pulp—literally. The beauty, the wholeness of the fruit appears destroyed. Certainly, if it could, the branches would protest. But from this crushing, the juice comes forth, the essence of the vine— its very life.

My heart is filled with gratitude that the Vine, the Lord Jesus, allowed His life to be smashed for me. He was crushed; His blood poured out, that we might drink of the cup of salvation—the Holy Wine!

Wine Making

I drink Your cup—Your Wine, Lord—
Rich symbol of Your Blood.
Your smitten Life was crushed, poured forth
Before I understood.
My clustered grapes—this fruit, Lord,
My "branch" formed through the Vine—
I feel them crushed. Lord, could this be
The way You make Your wine?

The First Blizzard of Winter

I truly respect You, Lord. I respect You even more than usual this morning as I watch winter tear past my window, sending snow sheets horizontally through the sky, then twisting them into mini-cyclones which dart and race among the apple trees in the orchard, now dimly seen through all this white fury. I watch with awe, and am thankful for our safe, warm log home.

I wonder who may be *out* in all this, far from being safe and warm, who may, in fact be in danger from the storm. I pray for them.

Lord, You are speaking through snow and tempest, through all the elements of Your world. You speak tenderness and gentleness through soft rains, warm sun, through delicate whispers of petunia fragrance on a summer night. But today You are speaking of Your power and the danger of being outside of proper shelter on the day of storm.

Storm warnings came yesterday, so this is no surprise. And, You have warned us in Your Word of stormy days ahead—economically, physically, and spiritually. May we heed those warnings and be ready.

You are our Refuge, Lord. You are our Safety. You, Lord, are our Shelter, our Dwelling Place. May none of us be caught "out" on a day like this!

In Jesus' Name.

The "Live" Tree

" . . .whatsoever things are lovely. . .think on these things."

(Philippians 4:8)

This morning the apple tree just outside my kitchen door was ladened with a flock of gorgeous Evening Grosbeaks. At least twenty-five of these handsome birds have come regularly to our bird feeder several times a day for the last few years. Each winter we look forward to their return and the day they arrive I feel like celebrating a reunion with old friends. All winter they will crowd and clamor after the sunflower seed in the feeder less than a foot away from my kitchen sink.

But this morning, en masse on my apple tree, they look-ed particularly magnificent. With brilliant gold and black and white markings on the male, and subtle putty-gold and black and white on the female, they transformed my old apple tree into a lavishly decorated "live" Christmas tree with chirping, live-bird ornaments. The bright morning sun spotlighted the white snow on the branches, which contrasted with the vivid color of the birds, adding to the spell of this magic tree, sparkling with snow diamonds and Evening Grosbeaks.

Then, in a moment, they flew away and the spell ended. But not really. For in my mind and memory I carry a snapshot of the image of those few seconds, or minutes, of "kairos." Clock time, "chronos," was irrelevant—it was "kairos"—high time—a "season" for watching grosbeaks.

We need such mental snapshots. The world has so much for us to watch which is not lovely, that our brain albums get filled with images of the mundane, the stupid, and the immoral. Too, there are countless cases of "overexposures"—snapshots where no image appears at all. Overly stimulated by the world's flashing strobe concepts, our cauterized sensibilities can fail to register the worthy and the beautiful.

Yet Scripture commands us to "think on" the things that are worthy and beautiful, to muse and meditate on the lovely. Herein lies one "ministry" of the arts—to supply us with sufficient material of "virtue and praise" that we not be hard pressed to come up with enough to "think on."

So while teaching art at The Stony Brook School, I used to urge my students to stop frequently during the day, or night, and take mental snapshots of moments of beauty—to pause long enough to savor and register the sights, sounds and fragrances which nature affords. I required them to hand in notebooks containing descriptions of these moments. For I believe that we become so preoccupied with what we have done—the past; and what we are about to do—the future, that we lose the "now." We look, but we do not see. Observation becomes a lost art.

Here in New England, I could fill untold numbers of notebooks with descriptions of sights and sounds and fragrances. Here, just my route to the grocery store takes me along old stone wall-lined pastures, through evergreen forests from which a lovely doe and her fawn once darted and crossed my path, past old farms with period homes of exquisite design, and beside steepled, white New England churches. Here, many mental snapshots of the beautiful are recorded daily.

But today—the prize winner—was of an old snow-ladened apple tree, alive with grosbeaks.

Lord, forgive our insensitivity to the beauty of Your creation. Thank you for every evidence of Your hand.

In Jesus' Name.

Playtime

"The Lord created me the beginning of his works ....
When he set the heavens in their place I was there,
when he girdled the ocean with the horizon ....
then I was at his side each day, ...
playing in his presence continually,
playing on the earth, when he had finished it ...."

Proverbs 8:22a, 27, 30a, 30c, 31a (NEB)

The earth invites play. This morning the snow is fluffy, light and new—waiting and welcoming the first who will step into its unmarked freshness. Such snow insists on frolic, and I can not help but respond; I jump into it, kick up my heels and dance a bit. It is impossible to walk a direct path from house to barn—the snow is too much like a spanking new white canvas, and the artist in me demands designs, not straight lines. So I swirl my paths, toss snow with my boots and create my snow- art with child-like abandon.

Mostly St. Bernard "Becky Bell" joins in—she, too, senses that it is play time, and she bounds towards me and then away, towards me and away—with snow flying in all directions. I snow-ball her, and she snow-showers me and we bark and laugh together.

I need such moments—times of release when I can allow the little girl in me to live. Having to act grown up *all* the time is too much for almost anyone, even for one hovering above the half-century mark.

Although making a god out of pleasure, as do the hedonists, is deplorable, there is the other extreme—forgetting how to play. This poses danger and deters the fullness of life in Christ which is our purchased inheritance. We can get too somber and go on duty-drives which by-pass the playground, thereby missing out on the re-creation which recreation is designed to give.

I know my own susceptibility to that temptation, and I am grateful for the help our farm gives me in this respect, offering me goats and kittens, beavers and Becky Bell, and mornings like this—all "youth-renewal" gifts from the Lord.

For I do believe that play is part of Divinity. I believe I hear the words of Christ in Proverbs, when "Wisdom" speaks. He is the "Wisdom of God," and I feel that here He is letting us in on the God Head's recreational activities, expressing His enjoyment of Creation, "playing on the earth when he had finished it." (NEB)

I wonder how He played. Did He romp in green pastures with little goat kids as I do with mine? Or in snow-covered ones with a happy dog companion? Did He walk beside beaver ponds and watch the beavers splashing their tails, diving and swimming their hardest for Him? Or did He swim Himself—diving into some sparkling pristine mountain lake? Did He ever ride a robust wave onto a sandy shore?

Did You, Lord? Did You ever play and dance in snow on such a morning as this?

> I'm so glad, as child of God,
>   My Daddy lets me play
>   Out in our yard—the world He made—
>   Until the close of day.

"God Rest You, Merry Gentleman"

Christmas here at our New Hampshire farm is always very special, beautifully blessed with our likeness to scenes depicted on Christmas cards—of snow-laden hills and trees, barn animals, and quaint New England villages.

Our most memorable Christmas since coming here was in 1984, Burt's Dad's last Christmas here on earth. Bone cancer had filled his pained body, but his heart and his disposition were merry. He was a "merry gentleman" this day, for he cared deeply for his family and he was thankful for this time of "remission" which was allowing us another Christmas together.

While Mom and I tended to indoor preparations, Burt and Dad braved the *minus* 20 degree cold and took tractor and wagon toward the ridge in search of a "home-grown" Christmas tree. The biting wind whipped the ridge and tall trees with no thought of mercy toward the undaunted Lauber men, to whom "difficulty" and "challenge" are synonymous.

They found their difficulty—they found their tree—a forty-foot tall spruce, standing high in the winter wind like the mast of a tall ship. Burt shinnied up the mast, and cut the top ten feet of the huge spruce, then loaded it, and loaded Dad on top of it, into the wagon which he then pulled home with the tractor.

The picture of Dad, a "city boy" all his days, sitting—frigid with the cold—with bright apple-red cheeks—nestled amid a bushy spruce Christmas tree, being pulled, smiling!—in a wagon attached to a tractor, through snow-covered woods roads, back into the driveway of our log home—is a scene printed indelibly on my memory.

We installed and decorated the tree; we put a bright star at its peak; and we celebrated our Christmas joyfully.

Dad celebrated the following Christmas in the company of other family members—those godly ones who preceded him into the presence of the One represented by that star atop the huge spruce Christmas tree.

The star of Bethlehem which led the wise men, the "Star of Jacob" spoken of by old Balaam, the prophet, as One who would rise to rule, and the Morning Star with which Jesus identified Himself, as He claimed, "I am the bright and Morning Star,"—all confer significance and wonder to our Christmas symbol.

The Star holds challenge as well, for also Jesus said, "he that overcometh and keepeth my works unto the end, to him I will give power over the nations. . .and I will give him the Morning Star." (Revelation 2:26-28)

What does that mean? I only know that here at the farm, the morning star is my portion only if I am awake before daybreak. While the white pines atop our ridge appear as solid, dark silhouettes against the brightening sky, the radiant morning star appears dramatically on stage as the dazzling "star performer." The sleeping miss the show.

So, to keep awake spiritually, to overcome temptation and testing by the power of God, and to keep Christ's commandments obediently unto the end—be it to the end of one's life, as in Dad's experience—or to the end of the age—results in a stunning reward of magnitude and brilliance.

God, help us meet the challenge of the star. Help us not to slumber in our spirits, but to be wide awake and obedient to Your call.

By Your Spirit, and
In Your Name,
Lord Jesus.
Amen.

C O L O P H O N

This book is one of an edition of
six hundred fifty copies
printed and bound at Golden Quill Press,
in the year nineteen-hundred eighty-eight.
The text is set in a digital facsimile
of a typeface designed in 1540 by
Geofroy Tory's pupil, Claude Garamond,
on command of Francois I of France.
The text paper, Smyth-sewn in sixteen page signatures,
is S.D. Warren's sixty-pound basis acid-free
Olde Style, manufactured at Westbrook, Maine.

This infinity symbol ∞
represents Golden Quill's commitment to quality paper stock,
which will last several centuries,
and our cooperation with
The National Information Standards Organization, Washington, DC.

DATE DUE

HIGHSMITH   # 45220